LIVING
ON WATER

LIVING ON WATER

CONTEMPORARY HOUSES FRAMED BY WATER

[1] BUILT TO LOOK AT WATER

[2] BUILT ON WATER

[3] BUILT TO REFLECT WATER

Just as roads and streets define cities, water shapes our landscape. It descends from alpine terrain and transforms into meandering rivers, streams, and tributaries to become inland lakes, lochs, fjords, or seas, through deltas and marshlands toward the coast and, from there, into vast oceanic reserves. As water travels it moves at various speeds, adopts different characteristics, and forges a new relationship with each environment it becomes a part of. It comes as no surprise, then, that it is where water meets land—from archipelago islands to secluded beaches, riparian banks to craggy coastlines—that some of the most distinctive natural settings and contemporary residences can be found.

Architecture is underpinned by four core components: the wall, the roof, the window, and the door. Each of these are bound by a single common purpose—to act as a barrier between a controlled interior space and an altogether less predictable wilderness beyond. The act of building, therefore, has a rather conflictual relationship with water; dependent on location—be it the arctic north, tropical south, or any of the temperate climes in-between—snow and ice, rain, and atmospheric humidity are considered to be among the architect's greatest adversaries.

Where there is water, however, there is infinite scope for architectural innovation. At a moment in which vernacular building techniques across the world have largely been diluted into little more than hermetically sealed boxes, there is a small but significant contingent of dwellings to which a more sensitive approach has been favored. Here, the relationship between land, house, and water (lakes, rivers, oceans, and climatic conditions, such as mist, fog, rain, and snow) is a deliberate design decision.

For a building to converse with its context, it must be capable of responding to the challenges posed by its particular environment. Water is an ever-changing visual canvas, absorbing and reflecting all shades of color and able to transform from planar to sculptural in a moment. It is, in other words, mercurial; it can behave with sudden volatility as swiftly as it can become serene and still. Whereas quiet islands positioned deep within a forested archipelago might be suited to muted interventions, rugged wind-swept shorelines and their tempestuous atmospheric conditions might accommodate a more defiant design. These sorts of aesthetic and climatic considerations are crucial for those that sit in, on, or next to aqueous terrains.

The "golden troika" of water, landscape, and architecture can—when approached with conviction and a certain intelligence—lead to homes of elevated technical prowess and exceptional beauty, a formula that only a rarified few ultimately achieve. This book collates projects that accomplish just that. These are private residences that, through a variety of design concepts and techniques, and within radically different settings, consummately prove that water can become a building's best friend after all.

[1] BUILT TO LOOK AT WATER

Bodies of water—be they immeasurably large, quantifiably small, or in a state of constant motion—represent a particular sort of serenity. In the same way that open skies provide a sense of space and spaciousness, unbroken aqueous planes, such as lakes or seas, render a meditative point of focus and, in so doing, a recognition of the scale of a landscape. It makes perfect sense that it is here, at the intersection of terra firma and terra incognita—between land and the expanded horizon beyond—that people choose to build homes.

For an architect tasked with designing a house that specifically looks toward a body of water, the challenges are clear, if not nuanced. Although there is, more often than not, a striking view to take into consideration, there is even more to be mindful of: however remarkable a vista, for instance, the relationship between a house and a landscape requires a series of decisions to be made. These, which are themselves largely dependent on the specific context, the climate, and the aspirations of the client, might question to what extent the lifestyle of living so close to water be drawn (or not) into the home. How should natural light—which is often more brilliant when reflected—be filtered or cascaded inside?

The best homes, as the projects in this chapter demonstrate, challenge the dominance of their artificial presence in the context of natural landscapes. It is only when the ephemerality of life by the water—breezes, scents, and sounds—is folded into the design that a more rooted sense of belonging can emerge.

Camilo Rebelo + Susana Martins
KTIMA HOUSE
2014 | Antiparos, Greece

Located on the island of Antiparos in Greece, Ktima House—which translates from the Greek as "a parcel of fertile land"—is a partially subterranean villa facing the sea. Appearing from its land-side entrance as little more than a thick, angular wall and a constellation of small elements peppering the dry, grassy landscape, the house disguises its size by subtracting itself from the landscape. It is, in many ways, an extension of the lines and walls that the architects originally found on the steeply sloping site, extended and manipulated into a deceptively large summer residence.

The composition and layout of the house allow for almost every room to have views toward the water and access to expansive patios, while remaining cool during the hottest hours of the day. The green roof, which blends into the flora of the landscape, is fundamental to the interior's temperature regulation. Light wells, emerging from the ground, allow for cross ventilation of the rooms.

On the western edge of Lake Garda, Italy, Villa Eden perches with a steadfast sense of its own gravitas atop a steep slope overlooking Gardone Riviera. While a delicate loggia of slender columns—a pergola of sorts, characteristic of local *limonaias* (lemon groves)—provides a shaded spot to look toward the water, the house itself extends as a solid formal expression of concrete and stone—the latter hewn from local quarries.

Inside, the favored material is wood, lending an altogether softer interior atmosphere. The living areas and bedrooms all face the water, while service rooms are located in the less-visible rear of the building. The quarters all connect to a long patio and pool that face the water and a patchwork of cypress trees.

decaArchitecture
VORONOI'S CORRALS
2012 | Milos, Greece

Located on a large, protected nature estate on the Greek island of Milos, Voronoi's Corrals is a house with a primitive quality. Positioned carefully to take advantage of breezes, the movement of the sun, the sounds of the water, and the existing vegetation, the house grew from a concept of a simple grid based on the ideas of Russian mathematician Georgy Voronoy.

Isolated atop a cliff edge, the house is built from limestone blocks, which form a gleaming white canopy. Similar to a primordial shell, the roof slants downward from a central keystone, diminishing the mass of the roofline and thereby anchoring a small courtyard in the center of the knot of rooms. Set amid an orchard of olive trees, vines, and herbs—all protected by a winding drystone wall—the house's direct engagement with the vegetation and the sea speaks of the resident's intent to blur the threshold between an indoor and outdoor life.

FALL HOUSE
2011 | Big Sur, CA, USA

Perched almost 262 feet (eighty meters) above the Pacific on a verdant cliff face, this house in California is composed of two volumes joined together by a glazed atrium that serves as a library and central meeting point, with the smaller of the two buildings cantilevered toward the ocean.

An open-plan interior sets the tone of the house, which is at once transparent and secluded. Level changes within demarcate the different living spaces, creating nested moments that speak to the water below. Terraces and patios occupy the boundary of the property, which is also home to a delicate ecosystem. As part of the sustainable approach to this residence, local and drought-resistant vegetation has been planted to reduce soil erosion and encourage wildlife to settle on the building's isolated site.

CASA DEL ACANTILADO
2012 | Alicante, Spain

The Casa del Acantilado, located in Calp, Alicante, in Spain, is a house defined by a series of strong formal moves. Hefty blank walls of white, coupled with a vast, gravity-defying cantilever, characterize a house that plays with its own structural dexterity while, at the same time, deferring to the sharp topography of its challenging site. Positioned at the top of a tall coastal hill, a large horizontal slab—utterly monolithic in appearance—directly faces the sea and, on each side, the peripheral harbor lights along the shore.

The entrance staircase, in a game of light and shade, ascends from a terrace and pool up along one side of an expansive structural wall, before puncturing through and continuing beneath the cantilever. Inside, the house maintains a clean and minimalist character, pulling focus to the windows, which look onto rocky outcrops or out toward the sea.

Submerged within a steep hillside near Granada, Spain, this house has an unconventional facade. To be perched on a forty-two-degree angled cliff, an ordinary house might need to make several concessions—stand taller, for instance, or incorporate needlessly large apertures into its facade—in order to take advantage of the spectacular views across the Mediterranean Sea. But this spacious, light-filled house lies behind a "scaled" exterior, a geometrically complex concrete shell constructed using a handcrafted formwork system in the shape of a metallic mesh. Zinc tiles complete the roof, sealing it off from the elements. The apparently modest size of the house belies its other, more surprising function. The main living space can be reconfigured into an auditorium, able to seat seventy or—in a pinch—even more people for larger parties. Events can also spill over onto the generous terrace, replete with a pool and astonishing views along the coast and toward the sea.

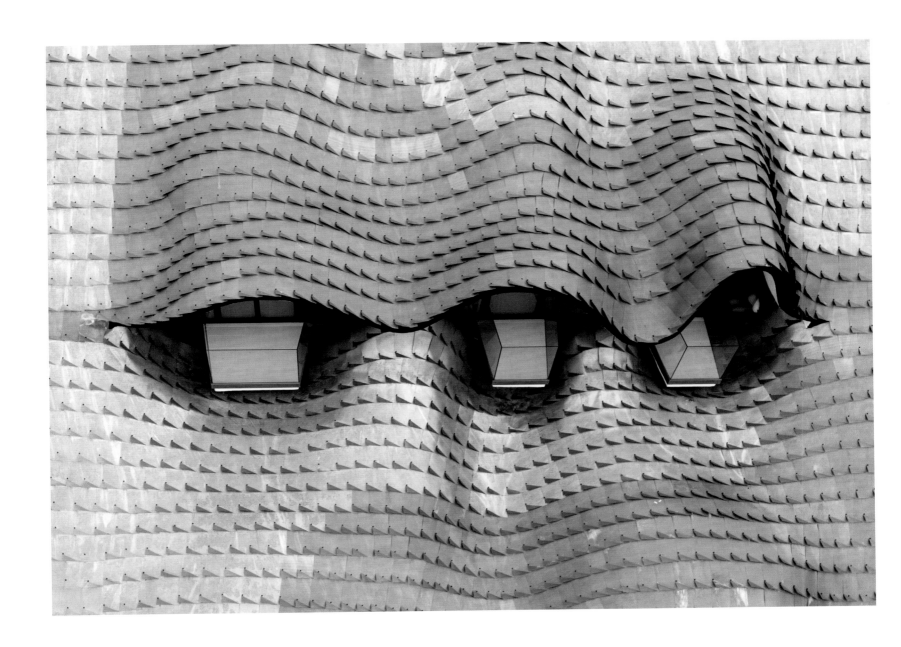

Located near Cachagua on the Chilean Tunquen coast, the Casa Mirador is a summer residence designed for its architect. The house recalls one of architectural history's seminal projects—the Villa Savoye in Poissy, France, which was designed by Le Corbusier in the 1930s as a manifesto for the Modernist movement. One key difference, however, is in its material finish—this project, recalling the craggy coastline on which it sits, is defined by exposed board-marked concrete.

With two elevated terraces looking out across land and sea simultaneously, the building stands assertively. Inside, however, the living spaces are altogether warmer and less brutal in character. Natural light floods in from above, while windows frame the surrounding views.

Nestled within a steep cliff face, the Silver House—sited on the Spanish coast, close to Girona—is a concrete edifice that appears to be cast into the very rock it sits on. A series of volumes, each appearing to emerge directly from the ground, collectively form a private residence that cascades down the slope, creating a sequence of terraces and shaded courtyards.

With apertures pointing toward the Mediterranean Sea and the rocky outcrops of the cliff, the house plays with its exterior spaces in unique ways. The landscape is allowed to encroach on the terraces, creating a striking contrast to the otherwise pristine white interiors. A staircase leading down to a lower terrace is itself hewn from the rock face; it can be read, in other words, as a subtraction of stone as opposed to an addition of space.

LAND Arquitectos
CATCH THE VIEW HOUSE
2013 | Zapallar, Chile

This house, positioned on the shore near Zapallar, Chile, embodies a very particular type of energy. Volumes of varying scales bisect each other to sprawl toward the water's edge, attempting—as its name suggests—to catch the views that lie beyond. The design of the house was based on a study of said vistas, while ensuring that the structure does not interfere with a nearby breakwater and a shallow ravine.

Prefabricated concrete panels that were assembled on-site construct a building able to take on the force of coastal weather. Sealed off from the natural elements by large glazed panels, the expansive interior of the house is treated in a bright white, with dark wood floors throughout. Whatever the time of day, these spaces are able to catch the varying light as well as the view.

HOUSE AT GOLEEN
2009 | Spanish Cove, County Cork, Ireland

The House at Goleen, near the coastal town of Spanish Cove, County Cork, is set in an area of renowned natural beauty. With the Celtic Sea just across the cliff, the house sits adjacent to a small stream. Mimicking the characters of speed and serenity possessed by these bodies of water, the house itself is composed as a collection of linear pavilions forming pockets of space and enclosed courtyards, each leading to a terrace with views directed to the sea and the islands of West Cork.

Clad in Irish blue limestone, each pavilion expresses a connection with its neighbor —and with the ground. Over time, each will weather to a tone that matches the formations of the nearby cliffs and—when wet—becomes dark and reflective.

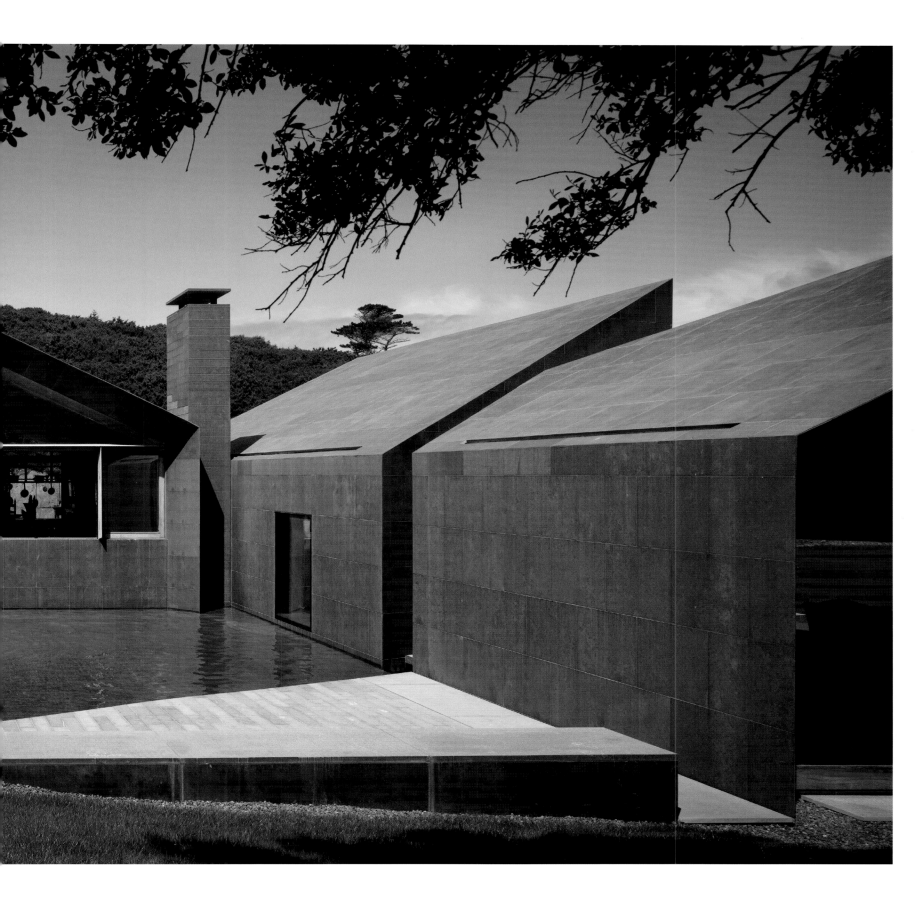

HOUSE IN BRISSAGO
2013 | Brissago, Switzerland

On the Swiss-Italian border, Brissago is a small town by the edge of a vast alpine lake. This house, a washed-concrete monolith of interlocking square panels, sits high above the water and rises out of the steep topography of its sloping site. A passageway leads visitors to the entrance, through which sit a secluded courtyard and simple olive grove.

The living areas, constructed with precision, have a similarly granular material character. Large windows with deep recesses are punctured through the walls to frame views across the lake and the mountains beyond; these picture windows, which stretch the full height of the interior rooms, also flood the spaces with natural light. A separate plinth, positioned farther down the site, accommodates a terrace and a pool, which directly overlook the water below.

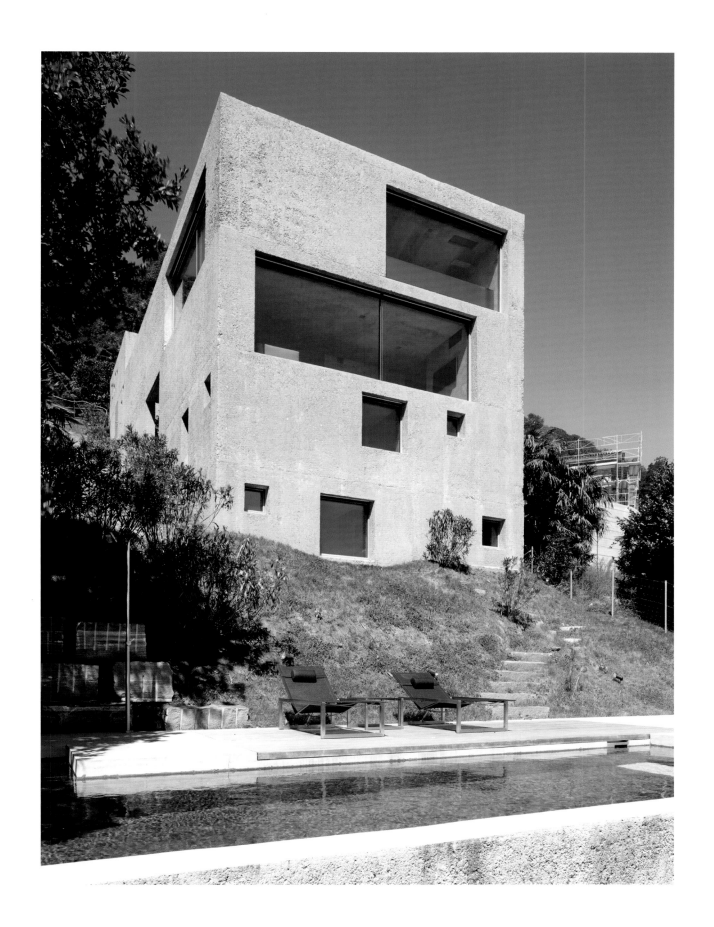

Do House, located in Los Vilos on the coast of central Chile, is a fortresslike residential villa. Perched on a rocky beach facing the Pacific, it is, on the one hand, defensive—shielding against the potential onslaught of the ocean—and, at the same time, calm and built with a remarkable level of precision.

A circular concrete wall—mimicking two protective arms—delineates the boundary of the house, while a bridged pathway from the entrance of the estate bisects the building and points out toward the sea. Inside, almost every wall surface, soffit, and ceiling is expressed in exposed concrete, while the floor is layered with wood. Two large glazed walls—one facing the sea, and the other facing land—flood the tall interior spaces with natural light and offer wide views of the expanded horizon.

The Jellyfish House, located in Marbella on the Spanish Mediterranean coast, is a dexterous attempt to fuse high-living with the presence of water and, in this case, swimming. The house itself, sculpturally formed from a precisely engineered concrete shell, is anchored around a pool—the base of which is constructed out of glass to allow filtered natural light to descend through turquoise water and onto an outdoor terrace. More impressively, perhaps, the pool is suspended by a thirty-foot (nine-meter) cantilever—a quite exceptional technical accomplishment for a house of modest size.

The interiors are characterized by polished white concrete and glazed surfaces, which take on a light-green tint. The roof—from which the pool can be accessed—affords views across the Sierra Blanca mountain range and the sea below. While the house presents itself as transparent, even voyeuristic, it is in fact a sealed private residence—showing itself to others but designed, in many ways, to be as private as possible.

Located on a Greek island and positioned on a gently sloping, verdant shoreline, the first Paros House—part of a sequence of "Cycladic" homes arranged on south-facing plots looking out at the sea—is a pristine white villa of relatively humble proportions. Its rectilinear volumes, which are arranged atop a concrete platform of a similarly orthogonal disposition, are encircled by rocks, yellow sand and dust, and shrubbery; it is, in other words, an oasis at the heart of a hot, empty landscape. An open-air terrace directs views toward the sea and neighboring islands.

This house is defined by a careful articulation of natural light and shadow. The way the light falls on the planar surfaces of the house reflects the Aegean sun, while deep recesses and shutters in the windows ensure that the heat of the day stays away from the interior spaces, keeping them cool during the arc of the afternoon and open toward the evening breeze.

Located at the edge of Loch Dunvegan in Scotland's Isle of Skye, Cliff House is a residence built for a couple with an ambition to escape into solitude. Conceived as two individual, low-lying interconnected volumes, the house is nestled on top of a gently sloping hill and almost entirely hidden from the land-side view. A winding pathway leads visitors down to the threshhold, whereupon an unobtrusive entrance guides them inside.

Larch, Caithness stone, and polished concrete form the core material palette for the exterior of the house. Inside, however, the spaces are comparatively Spartan, designed to focus attention on the view and on the personal collections of its residents. The voids between the two volumes are glazed, providing vistas out to the water and offering backward glances to the building's larger setting. They also signal the material shifts that define the character of the residence and its relationship to the landscape at large.

When the footprint of a house requires a minimal impact on its surroundings, an architect is left with precious few options. In the case of Pole House, located on Australia's Great Ocean Road, the solution was simple: position the house atop a forty-two-foot (thirteen-meter) column protruding from a sloping hillside stretching down toward a beach.

A bridge connects the house to the land, passing over a canopy of trees. The plan, which is simply an offset square, is defined by two facades open with windows (those facing the ocean) and two entirely closed (those facing land). The house itself is modest in scale, designed primarily to focus its residents on the scenic views of the ocean and distant coastline. From its elevated position, it commands its landscape with a watchful, if not steadfast, gaze.

Positioned on the banks of the glacial river Hvítá, east of the Icelandic capital of Reykjavík, this low-lying single-story house sits on a moss-covered rural site, looking out across the still water. Clad in concrete mixed with gravel aggregate from the pier below, the exterior walls are inscribed with vertical lines, lending them an almost pre-historic character—as if excavated from a granite cave.

Inside, the house is defined by sharp, clean lines and precise construction. Concrete walls complement wood-paneled floors and ceilings—creating spaces that feel as though, if left alone, they could embrace and fuse with the landscape beyond. A large cantilever balances the building's biggest volume over the riverbank, bestowing upon it a sense of weightlessness.

With a ground plan shaped like a tulip flower, El Ray is a beach house with a direct view toward the English Channel. Located in Kent, United Kingdom, not far from the Dungeness power station, the site was formerly occupied by a re-used railway carriage. This house is its replacement, designed to accommodate a family of permanent residents.

The old railway carriage is, in fact, positioned inside El Ray's living area, facing a glazed south elevation looking across the water. The house around the carriage has been constructed using a highly insulating timber structure, ensuring the building is cool in the summer months and warm in the winter. The habitable roof deck allows for panoramic views of the low-lying landscape around—which is often prone to strong and unexpected gusts. Two enclosed courtyards built into the tulip-shaped plan act as windbreaks.

Tham & Videgård Arkitekter
SUMMERHOUSE LAGNÖ
2012 | Lagnö, Sweden

Located in the Stockholm archipelago, this Swedish summer house, built atop a concrete plinth and facing a bay, appears from a distance like a collection of vernacular, gabled-roof homes. The bedrock of the archipelago is granite, and the house, with its gray finish and weighty composure, is designed to appear as if it had been fused immovably with the ground it occupies.

A sequence of four gabled roofs—forming two buildings—are connected by a glazed, pitched canopy. Referencing vernacular boathouses, the ceiling heights inside are low. Warm, wood-lined interiors face a continuous sliding door that opens out toward the water, while polished concrete floors delineate the threshold between interior, exterior, and interstitial (the terrace) space. A separate building closer to the water's edge accommodates a sauna.

Built at the water's edge on a site near Bergen, Norway, Villa Tyssøy is a striking structure of two bright-white volumes in an otherwise sparsely populated natural environment. Angled lines converge to create a single, abstract block; horizontal elements and curved edges unite to create a building that is at once bold and yet deferent to the scale of the landscape it sits within.

From the water, the house emerges from the top of a grassy knoll, while expansive windows frame views back down toward the sea. Inside, a collection of modestly sized rooms—all painted white—take advantage of the clear Norwegian light to lend the interior a sense of space. Simply orchestrated, they appear to absorb their surroundings.

[2] BUILT ON WATER

History has served contemporary architects a range of models for building on water, from traditional fishing homes to more audacious prospects of floating villas. However, it presents an inherent—if not poetic—paradox. As a result, houses able to successfully bridge the space between solid earth and liquid land are few and far between—but, as the projects collected in this chapter attest, almost always remarkable. To work successfully they must reconcile structure, design, and functionality to tread the fine (and sometimes indistinguishable) line between a house that is merely a pleasure to look at and one that is also a joy to live in.

For this reason, designs for these types of schemes are often unconventional by necessity, rather than by choice. To harmonize an unmoving object in space with an altogether less robust natural element requires innovative techniques and approaches to design—and not only in terms of construction. In some cases, a house must become the shore or coastline, a riverbank or jetty, and thereby assume the role of a piece of landscape rather than simply acting as an element within it. Yet, as can be seen by the range and craft of houses presented in this chapter, when a challenge such as this is posed, the results can be spectacular.

Alberto Morell
TULIA HOUSE
2015 | Kilifi, Kenya

Tulia House, located in Kilifi, Kenya, is set on a three-acre (1.2-hectare) plot between a mangrove and a coral cliff, facing the Indian Ocean. Because of the hot and humid climate, the building's proximity to the water allows for it to be naturally ventilated, thereby requiring minimal energy.

The house itself is defined by a large platform, in which a thirty-foot-wide (nine-meter-wide) staircase descends like an incision. At the foot of the staircase sits a secluded plunge pool, from which the sounds and scents of the nearby ocean can be felt—but not seen. The building was constructed using inexpensive materials—concrete, coral stones quarried close by, and, externally, stucco. The interior rooms, which are primarily on the upper floor, are defined by wooden screens and "diaphragms" that carve and compartmentalize the spaces.

Located on a smooth, rocky descent toward the sea near Helsinki, Finland, this summer house—described as a glazed pavilion—is modest in size. Positioned between a pine forest and the water, it sits parallel to the shoreline and is designed to be as unobtrusive as possible.

A large, undulating roof—which follows the topography of the site—creates grand eaves that serve as shelter from the sun, rain, and prevailing winds. The protected terraces, cast in concrete and lined with wood, complement the interior material palette, which is defined by oak wood, limestone, and copper. A sparsely furnished but intelligently organized sequence of rooms allow for almost every space to have panoramic views of the water.

Built around a series of shallow ponds that flow out from the Yellowstone River, Watershed Lodge appears as a collection of intersecting planes and platforms—each shading the interior spaces and delineating the floors and rooms of the house. Located in Big Timber, Montana, the entire building sits on an elevated plinth to allow the waters that surround it to dilate and disappear as the hours and the seasons pass by.

Inside, the house looks out to its surrounding landscape in all directions. Light-filled living spaces are treated with hardwoods and highlighted by concrete elements, such as the sizable hearth. Wooden decks lead down to the water's edge and allow the landscape to be accessed from any part of the house.

MANSHAUSEN ISLAND RESORT
2015 | Manshausen, Norway

Located on a small island in the Steigen archipelago, northern Norway, these four compact residences house visitors taking advantage of the area's hiking, fishing, diving, and skiing. The buildings are connected to their surroundings, perched on a rocky breakwater facing the clear, cold waters of the Norwegian Sea. Clad in a pale timber and entirely glazed on the side facing the water, each cabin is positioned to maximize the water views while providing privacy from the others.

Inside, each minimalist interior is angled toward the view. Light and bright—designed to be occupied primarily in the summer months—the homes are defined by a modest character, which attests to the simple life to be led on the islands.

Refuge, in Flanders, Belgium, is a residence built on a parcel of farmland surrounded by a pond, reeds, and low-lying marshland. Built almost entirely of wood and constructed by a local master carpenter, the house appears to float on the water, anchored only by a connection to an existing brick building. The roof, covered with redwood shingles, collects rainwater through copper spouts and returns it to the pond.

Wood also takes predominance in the interior spaces, lining the floors and the ceiling to create a comfortable atmosphere. With doors able to open out toward the water, the permeable walls of the home represent a mediation between indoor and outdoor life. In such a changeable climate as that of Belgium, this represents a comparatively innovative approach to country living.

HOUSE OVER THE SEA
2014 | Surry, ME, USA

Located in Surry, Maine, this house has a rather precarious relationship with Blue Hill Bay, the body of water it overlooks. Erected on wooden piers, the single-story structure is, as a result, relatively unaffected by the tides or the gradual erosion of the shoreline. At the base of the columns—at the edge of the water—a south-facing terrace stands shaded by the building above.

While the house is open on three sides to the water, the land entrance area—in which the bathrooms and the kitchen are situated—is comparatively closed and clad in shingles, a locally traditional material. Inside, the house is colored in soft blues and greens to invoke the shades of its immediate surroundings.

This waterside house is unusual in its portability. Originally designed by students and academics at a Portuguese university, the modular structure—which is completely self-sustainable for up to a week—can be built on the world's most remote or inhospitable bodies of water.

Twenty feet (six meters) wide and between thirty-three and fifty-nine feet (ten and eighteen meters) long, depending on ambition and configuration, the residence has a distinctly maritime feeling—decked out in hardwoods and plywood to create a minimalist, functional interior. A roof terrace encourages elevated views across whatever body of water on which the house might be floating, while the deck at the front is rather unusually, but absolutely necessarily, kitted out with a steering wheel and power throttle.

SHEARERS QUARTERS

2011 | North Bruny Island, Tasmania, Australia

Built on a working sheep farm on Tasmania's North Bruny Island, the Shearers Quarters is a compact, low-lying residence positioned close to the water's edge. Located on the site of a former shearing shed and next to an existing cottage, the house is clad in pine wood and corrugated sheet metal, lending it an industrial feel.

Designed to house the sheep-shearers during the season, the house is furnished simply and with maximum effort to focus the interior on the landscape outside. The internal living spaces, therefore, have a direct and uninhibited view toward the sea. The bedrooms are lined with recycled wood—discarded apple crates, no less—that the architects sourced nearby.

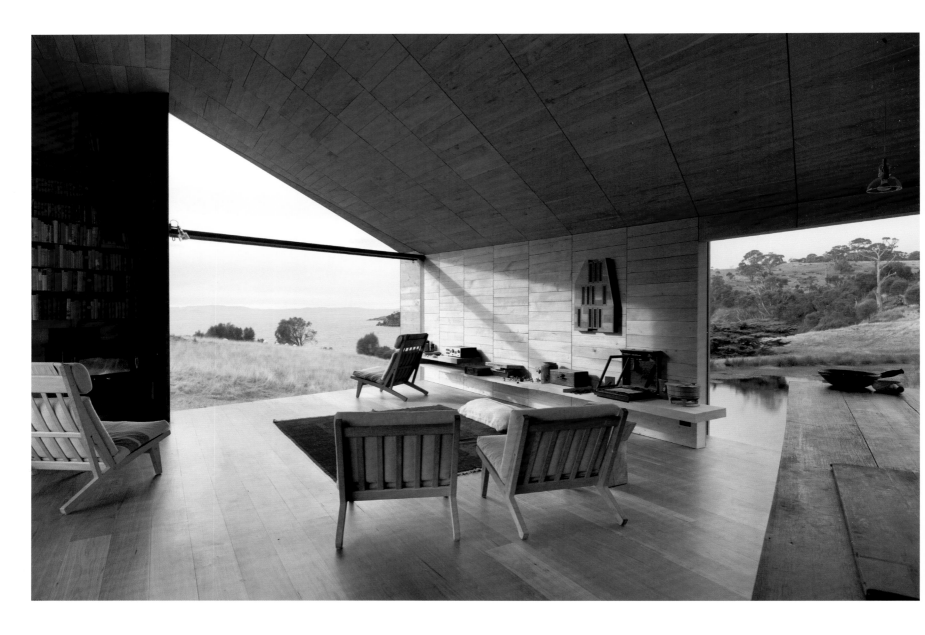

FLORIDA BEACH HOUSE
2011 | Palm Beach, Australia

Located in Palm Beach, Australia, Florida Beach House is a private residence on the coast of the Indian Ocean. A large sculptural roof with undulating peaks and troughs covers the sprawling home, the overhang of which is proportioned to keep the summer sun at bay while allowing in low-level winter sun. The distinction between interior and exterior is blurred by expansive vegetation. Decks, positioned on all four axes of the house, allow the residents to enjoy outdoor space at any time of the year.

Although the site reaches down to the beach, the house does not have direct views of the water. Through its form, however, the residence has been designed to recall the movement of the ocean—shimmering white and in a state of constant flux.

LOBLOLLY HOUSE
2006 | Taylors Island, MD, USA

Loblolly House, located on Taylors Island, Maryland, is, in essence, a tree house. Situated between a pine wood and a salt meadow stretching down to the water, the house is elevated on columns—all slightly askew—which are, as a result, camouflaged to blend in with the trees beyond. This creates a loggia of sorts beneath the building, enabling the breeze to circulate and allowing for elevated views across the bay. The living spaces inside have large glazed windows facing the water, each of which opens completely. At the core of the house is a footbridge connecting the main residence to guest quarters. Composed of tinted glass, this hearthlike structure takes on an orange glow when the sun moves west.

Cabin Lille Arøya, located in Larvik, Norway, is positioned on a small, rocky outcrop steps away from the water's edge. Accessible only by boat and entirely exposed to the natural elements, the house is spacious but low-lying—almost invisible from most parts of the island that it inhabits. Constructed of timber beams and galvanized steel columns, the building's structure is anchored directly to the rock.

Comprising two volumes, the house has a modest living area. The floor levels inside accommodate the topography of the site, giving the building an internal sequence that connects naturally to the landscape. The interior rooms, which look out to the sea, are defined by light woods and textured concrete, lending the spaces a warm, bright atmosphere.

STUPET REFUGIUM BY A STAIRCASE
2013 | Vättern, Sweden

Perched precariously on a cliff edge in Vättern, near Omberg, Sweden, this house employs a collection of rustic materials to blend the appearance of the building with its surrounding landscape, composed primarily of rock and woodland. The thresholds sit at the level of the topography of the site, while the interior spaces flow seamlessly toward the cusp of the cliff and the water down below.

This house is, in other words, an attempt to blur the boundaries between tame interior space and the rugged natural landscape by means of subtle aesthetic and structural moves. A very minimal distinction between the wall and roof, for instance, ensures that the building feels and appears to be a single, coherent project.

This simple residence, located in Letterfearn, Kintail, Scotland, sits on the edge of a loch against the backdrop of the Five Sisters mountain range. A traditional pitched-roof structure with a facade of glazing protrudes on the water's edge, opening up expansive views from the interior living spaces. Connected to an existing house, and mimicking its proportions, the project blends new and old in a seamless, if not entirely contemporary, way.

Inside, a staircase connecting the ground and upper floors is open to the overhead view by means of a large skylight. The various apertures allow the bright light of the Highlands to flood inside, illuminating the white interiors and the occasional walls clad in timber of the living spaces.

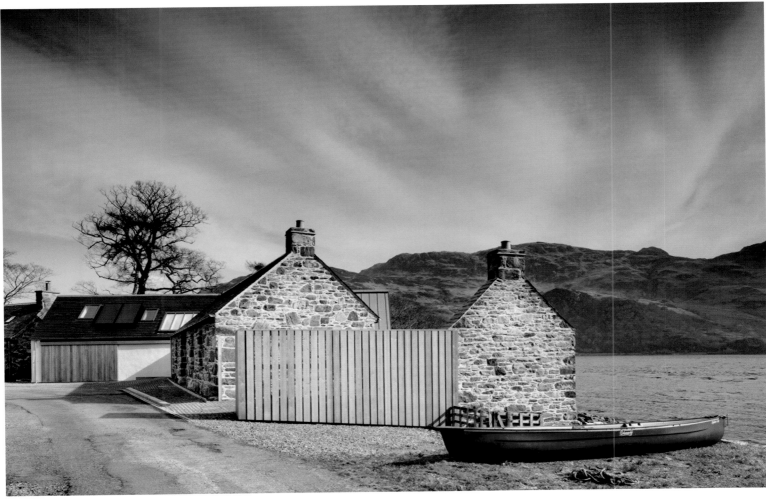

Sited on the Beaulieu River—formerly known as the River Exe—in the New Forest, United Kingdom, the Exbury Egg is a remarkable artistic endeavor designed to explore ways of living in natural landscapes. This floating residence, which is intended to have as minimal an impact on its environment as possible, was apparently inspired by the seabirds that nest on the banks of the waterway.

Built by a local boat builder, the egg was constructed as a cold-molded reclaimed cedar-sheathed structure. Inside, the living space is small and perfectly formed—there is room for a hammock (ideal, no doubt, in a floating house), a desk, a small stove, and an oval-shaped skylight for viewing the sky.

FLOATING HOUSE
2005 | Lake Huron, Ontario, Canada

On an isolated island in Lake Huron, Ontario, this house is designed to cope with a rather harsh seasonal weather system. Positioned on an inlet, the house acts as a bridge, connecting two sides of the bay by means of a walkway. Built almost entirely of wood—aside from its steel structure and floating apparatus—the house references local vernacular architectural styles. In so doing, its symmetrical facade is at once understated and surprisingly unconventional.

Large windows on the upper floor look out toward the lake. Inside, a simple interior directs attention to the surrounding view, defined by rocky outcrops, woodland, water, and the expansive horizon.

Located on Shelter Island, New York, this compact house is positioned on a bank of sand dunes, close to the water's edge. A series of terraces gather around a narrow pool, which faces out toward the bay and is screened from public view by plantings of native grasses. The outdoor area is defined by a long wall of cedar, painted black, that separates the driveway from the entrance.

A series of spaces designed to take advantage of the water views compose the living quarters. The colorful interiors, with wooden floors and ceilings, contribute to the residence's informal character. In the main living space, a large circular hearth dominates the room, which makes the most of the clear oceanic light.

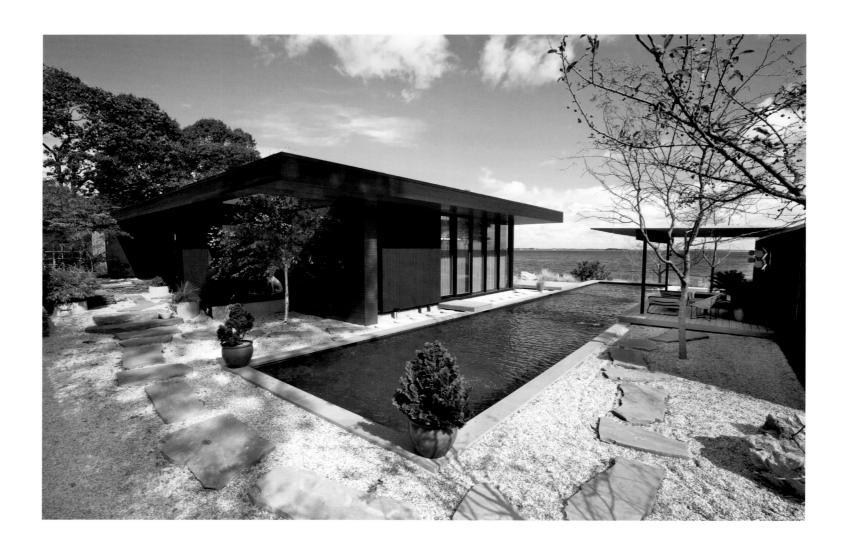

BLANKPAGE Architects (Karim Nader,
Patrick Mezher, and Walid Ghantous)
AMCHIT RESIDENCE
2014 | Amchit, Lebanon

Los Vilos, Chile, is known for its majestic, craggy coastline. Casa Bahia Azul has been designed to sit on a gently sloping outcrop that, in turn, descends toward the ocean. From the outside, the house appears off-kilter and unstable—as though only standing because it has been balanced between two rocks. This outward appearance belies a more conventional interior, however, in which sleek spaces—finished in concrete and stone—look out to the water below.

This house disguises itself. Composed of an intelligent combination of corridors and apertures, rooms and open courtyards, the house is defined by the slope it sits on— but simultaneously defines that slope, too. Set against the backdrop of a broken ridge of rocks, it has a purity of presence; a testament, perhaps, to architecture's capacity to reorder our surroundings.

ROCK HOUSE
2009 | Vestfold, Norway

Located on the shore at Vestfold, near the Norwegian capital of Oslo, stands Rock House: a project with heritage. Built on the site of a former dwelling, and incorporating a set of existing stone walls, the house was required by its permits to be sensitive to the topography of the land, as well as to its appearance in the setting. To achieve this, the house is clad in Kebony wood—a treatment that maintains its durability against corrosive saltwater.

The design is a low-slung, elongated structure that faces the water. The careful shaping of its volumes allows for exterior areas to be shielded from harsh winds, creating pockets of habitable outdoor rooms. The stone walls were extended using rocks blasted on-site, forging a strong material connection between the house and the surrounding cliffs. In spite of its protective demeanor, however, Rock House also manages to maximize views out toward the fjord.

SUNSET ROCK HOUSE
2011 | Shag Harbour, Nova Scotia, Canada

Located on the southern coast of Nova Scotia, Canada, Sunset Rock House has a large presence and a small footprint. Shaped like a blade poised above the ocean, the main volume of the house is elevated above the ground on a sequence of slender concrete fins. It is specifically oriented due west in order to catch the sun as it sets beneath the horizon.

Constructed by local boat builders, the house has a distinctly nautical atmosphere. Clad in gray corrugated metal sheeting and marine-grade plywood, the house is built to withstand various weather conditions. During heavy fog—which frequents the site regularly—the building often disappears behind a sheath of mist; at dawn and dusk, its profile marks the landscape much like a ship cast adrift.

[3] BUILT TO REFLECT WATER

Since time immemorial, architects have played with the combined qualities of light and water, and often to breathtaking effect. The Italian city of Venice, among the most accomplished examples of a "floating architecture," chose to face the challenge of its environment—which was, when initially settled, little more than mosquito-infested marshland—by constructing edifices of an awe-inspiring level of ingenuity and functionality. There, in the still mimetic pools of Turner, Monet, and Canaletto, horizons appear unanchored as buildings dissolve between the two broad expanses of the water and the sky.

When positioned near a body of water, therefore, a house is required to be more acutely aware of the impact of its presence; amplified and all the more dramatic, a mirrored image is almost a truer reflection of a bearing on a landscape. Light takes on a different intensity, too, as do acoustic patterns, and the shape and volume of the building—how much or how little it complements or obscures its surroundings—becomes a profoundly important consideration.

While approaches might differ among sites and clients, an architect's conscious effort to deftly engage with water by means of reflection, itself constantly shifting and mutating, is an ambition to be lauded. As revealed in this chapter, a project that is able to achieve this singular goal often deploys a broad range of techniques, articulating materiality, proportion, and views in order to synthesize itself with its habitat. To build a house that reflects on water is to embrace architecture's role in the ever-changing nature of a landscape.

The Domus Aurea (House of Gold) in Monterrey, Mexico, is a light-filled residence designed as a contemporary homage to Luis Barragán, the late Mexican architect who has come to symbolize aspects of the nation's architectural character. Colored a pristine white both inside and out, aside from the grand statement of a single golden surface, the house is a manifestation of a rather doctrinal way of living, defined by clean, orthogonal lines and a profound purity of space.

Finished to an exceptionally high quality, the house has an entrance from the street marked by a marble-lined vestibule. Here, on the ground floor, are public spaces of the residence; on the upper floor, more private spaces look down to the courtyards, terraces, and a swimming pool, which performs as a reflecting pool at the heart of the house. Enclosed by a wall, an aperture allows for views toward the urban environment beyond.

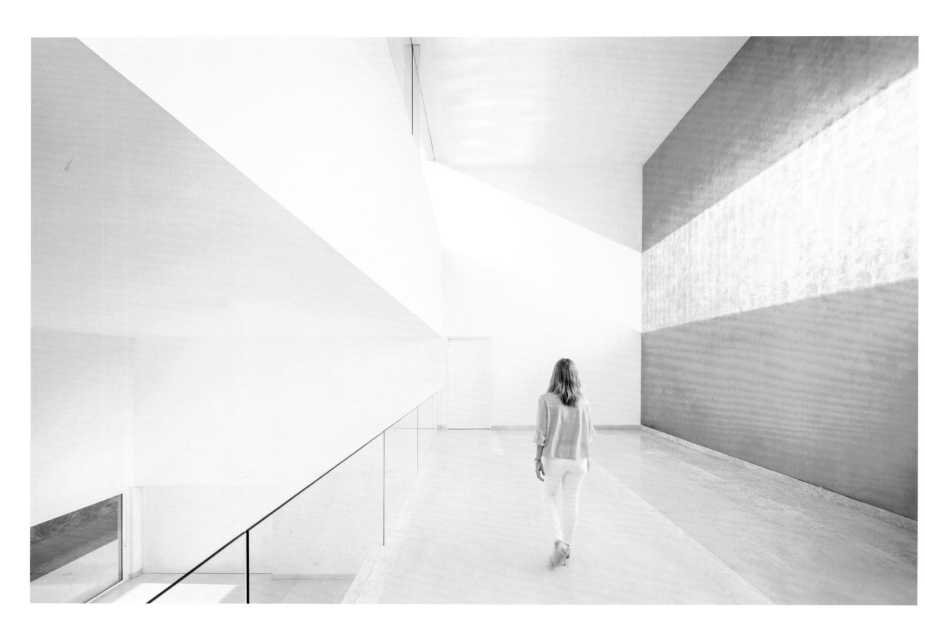

This single-family residence and guest house, located in Newberg, Oregon, sit at the heart of a wooded reserve facing an artificial pond. Tall trees surround the unobtrusive, low-lying volume of the house—which is itself built primarily from treated wood.

Entrance to the house is from a bridge that passes over a shallow body of water. Inside, the spaces are modest and warm. Tall glazed walls, made taller by an angled roof, look out toward the water. The stately, long reflecting pond, built in the tradition of landscaped northern European gardens of the nineteenth century, allows for precise and expansive reflections. It is in this surface that the house, the sky, and the nearby trees coalesce into a singular, idyllic vision of country living.

DAMA ZAMYA VILLA
2010 | Phuket, Thailand

Built on a remote island near Phuket, Thailand, the Dama zAmya Villa is designed to be entirely self-sufficient; a well provides its water supply, while renewable energy sources provide the electricity. Facing the ocean to the north and rainforest to the south and east, the building itself is defined by two separate living quarters bridged by a pool and a terrace. A grass-covered roof allows it to blend into its surroundings while simultaneously cooling its microclimate.

The ocean views are carefully constructed for maximum effect. Although not immediately visible, the water is revealed through the attentive orchestration of walls, windows, and the carving of the landscape. There is from the main living spaces on the upper level of the house, however, a full view of the ocean and the far horizon. A still pool accessible from a terrace sits high above the carpet of green below, reflecting the bold architectural moves that define the villa's contemporary character.

Skywood House, located in Middlesex, United Kingdom, is the very image of a sleek, minimalist home straight out of Hollywood. Positioned between a large, dark swimming pool and an artificial lake, the house is, in essence, a large-scale exploration of geometric space, glass, and the ambiguity of reflected surfaces.

Precisely constructed, the house has a polished limestone floor that extends from interior space to exterior, and then back again. This continuous off-white surface provides—like much of the gleaming white surfaces throughout—a canvas for shadows to settle and disperse. Beneath the canopies of brise-soleil, light and shade are bisected to create rigorous, orthogonal lines. Here, transparency is treated as a craft rather than a by-product.

Located in Chowara, Kerala, India, the Cliff House is a spacious residence designed to make the most of what is an intense tropical climate. Positioned to have a panoramic view across the Arabian Sea, the house is set high upon a steep escarpment, with the spaces orchestrated around a large reflecting pool and surrounded by a dense coconut plantation.

Built to ensnare the warm breezes that flow in from across the sea, the house is defined by a long skewed concrete wall that supports a light canopy roof. Slate, Kota stone, and timber paneling create a rich interior material palette, which offers balance to the home's minimalist aesthetic. The pool, appearing to pour over the edge of the cliff, is designed to mirror and flex the building's hard geometric angles.

THE HOUSE CAST IN LIQUID STONE
2013 | Khopoli, Maharashtra, India

This house, located in Maharashtra, India, is a spatial diagram of carefully considered tropical living. Built upon a basalt ridge, the building is designed to appear as if risen from within the earth. Its primary material, concrete, is blended with granular basalt as aggregate, lending the house its strikingly dark appearance.

Built to cope with the specific climatic challenges of its site—namely, monsoons and a considerably humid atmosphere—the living spaces of the house are collectively orchestrated to harness the natural elements and,

in addition, to take in the surrounding views. Defined by a sequence of shaded living areas and courtyards, the house has an upper terrace that culminates in a pool, reflecting the changing colors of the sky while addressing, by mirroring, the mountainous landscape beyond.

HOUSE IN MONTERREY
2011 | Monterrey, Mexico

Located in the Cumbres de Monterrey National Park, this house—designed by acclaimed Japanese architect Tadao Ando—is a summer retreat. Set against the backdrop of undulating topography and craggy cliff faces, this concrete building, positioned halfway up a hillside, projects its angular volumes out toward a swimming pool, which cantilevers over the edge of a sharp slope.

Divided into two wings and arranged around a double-height library space at the center of house, the building is minimalist in character. A shallow reflecting pool occupies a highly visible, open courtyard at the heart of the building, while carefully positioned windows, coupled with fully glazed walls, offer views of the dry, hot landscape.

TYAGI'S RESIDENCE

2006 | Bangalore, India

Located in Bangalore, India, Tyagi's Residence—named after its client and occupant—comprises a collection of living rooms arranged around a central swimming pool. The form of the house itself, which is a complex composition of intersecting planes and surfaces, moves to simplify internally in order to create this hollowed void.

Views of the pool from the internal rooms are maximized. This body of water, therefore, is intended to "complete" the rooms—reflecting and extending their presence into the large central space. An intricate construction of skylights and shades bisects the light as it falls into the house, creating a sea of shifting rectilinear shadows that reflect the changing course of the day.

Villa Kogelhof, located in the southern Dutch coastal town of Kamperland, is a striking realization of a clear and distinct architectural concept. A single volume, elevated high above a rectangular reflecting pool, is the visible, floating half of the house. It is anchored by a subterranean volume. Standing at the heart of a twenty-six-acre (10.5-hectare) protected estate, the villa has an entirely open floor plan divided only by a series of glass rooms and dividers. In this house, visibility is paramount, both of the surrounding landscape and among spaces within. Being energy neutral and, in most ways, self-sufficient, the house affords a certain variety of stark, contemporary—if not luxury—living.

Takuro Yamamoto Architects
WHITE CAVE HOUSE
2013 | Kanazawa, Japan

White Cave House, located in Kanazawa, Japan, is a solid volume, hollowed out and articulated into a complex arrangement of interior spaces. Colored white both inside and out, the house is designed to benefit from the refracted light that pours into a central courtyard, itself completely enclosed from the street life.

The roof of the building, which is also designed to have an equally high level of privacy, is defined by an expansive, shallow reflecting pool. This body of water serves to provide two functions: reflecting the changing colors and movements of the sky, thereby breaking the monotony of the incessantly white nature of the house and creating a cool and pleasant space for spending summer afternoons.

Perched atop a steep verdant cliff, this isolated house has a commanding view of the Balearic Sea—which sits a full 521 feet (159 meters) below its site. Strictly orthogonal in design and painted a bright white both outside and in, the house is defined by inner courtyards and secluded interior moments in which shelter from the bright Mediterranean sun can be found.

Approaching the house from the land, a staircase descends through a verdant, rocky outcrop. Inside, large windows frame views of the sea and simultaneously protect inhabitants from the often-strong winds that sweep up the coastline. Patios engage the interior spaces with the exterior, and a pool points toward the horizon while reflecting the architecture and the sky. From here, the tumult of the waves below is little more than a distant sound.

VILLA ÖVERBY
2009 | Värmdö, Stockholm, Sweden

Villa Överby is a Swedish summer house located in Värmdö, part of the Stockholm archipelago. The formal expression of the building is deceptively simple—a rectangular volume with views open on two sides to the sea. It is, however, the precision of its execution that sets it apart. In its effort to simplify and mask all potentially obtrusive elements (such as lights and ventilation), the villa has a remarkable sense of unity.

Built upon stone, which itself is anchored to the bedrock beneath, the house employs an elementary material palette of light-colored, durable materials. Limestone from Gotland, white ash, and pristine white surfaces combine to create an architecture that stands—in the middle of natural wilderness—as testament to the technical prowess of man-made construction.

At the edge of the outdoor terrace, a pool falls away toward the landscape, at once reflecting the skies and the house itself—signaling, perhaps, that the distinction may not in reality be so clear-cut.

Olson Kundig
POLE PASS RETREAT
2013 | San Juan Islands, WA, USA

Located in the San Juan Islands, Washington (near the Canadian border), Pole Pass is a modest retreat positioned at the edge of a forested shoreline facing out toward the Salish Sea. Because the summers in this region are climatically temperate, the glass walls of the main living space are made to roll completely open.

Designed to address both the woodland and the water, the house is striking in form. Responding to the vertical trees that surround the site and reflecting the horizontality of the water beyond, it is composed of flat roof surfaces beneath which sit a collection of open living spaces. When the glass walls are retracted, the boundary between interior space and the landscape is therefore blurred. To expand the notion of indoor/outdoor living, a preparation table extends from the kitchen out onto a decked patio.

This house, located in Victoria Beach, Canada, is geared wholly toward taking advantage of its exceptional lake view. Designed to mimic local vernacular architecture, which is defined by stone and wood-frame cottages, the building is low and slight, facing the water with an angular self-awareness.

A wall of windows opens out onto a spacious deck that descends to the beach, connecting the house to the water in just a few steps. Being slightly elevated above the level of the lake affords the deck panoramic views of the water and the dramatic weather conditions in this part of Canada. Clad in cedar planks, the house has an almost maritime quality and will, with age, transform in color from a rich red to a bright, whitish silver.

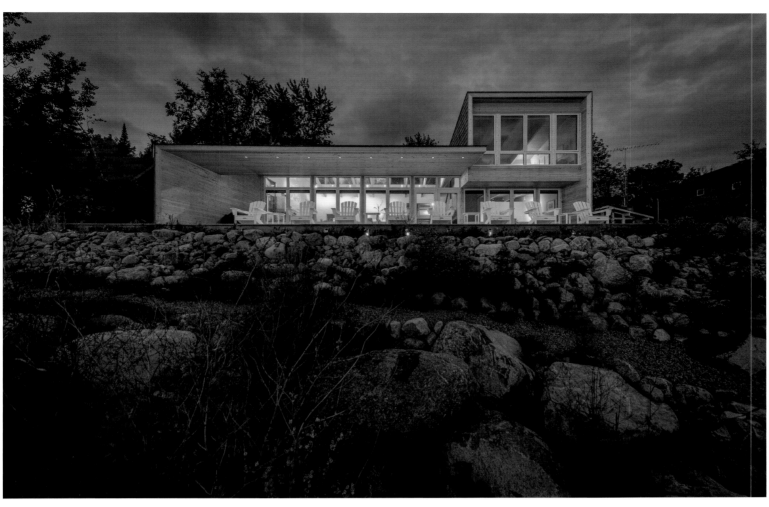

THE PUNTA HOUSE
2011 | Punta del Este, Uruguay

Positioned at the edge of a reservoir in Punta del Este on Uruguay's southern coast, this single-story house designed by Studio MK27 (Marcio Kogan and Suzana Glogowski), with interiors by Studio MK27 and Diana Radomysler, is characterized primarily by an orthogonal orchestration of walls, roofscapes, and spaces that seek to blur the distinction between interior and exterior space. Put simply, the house is formally composed of a flat exposed-concrete slab, beneath which sit the living and sleeping spaces, each enclosed in structures built of wood.

A local stone, known as *piedras lajas*, was used to construct the walls and floors, lending the house a rustic disposition. The addition of wild flora and other vegetation around the boundary of the building is part of the client's ambition to connect the residence with the surrounding landscape and the reservoir especially, in which reflections of dawn and sunset contribute to the house's wild nature.

Phaidon Press Limited
Regent's Wharf
All Saints Street
London N1 9PA

Phaidon Press Inc.
65 Bleecker Street
New York, NY 10012

phaidon.com

First published 2018
© 2018 Phaidon Press Limited

ISBN 978 0 7148 7572 9

A CIP catalogue record for this book is available from the
British Library and the Library of Congress.

Commissioning Editor: Emilia Terragni
Project Editor: François-Luc Giraldeau
Production Controller: Sue Medlicott and Nerissa Vales
Design: SJG/Joost Grootens, Julie da Silva,
    Silke Koeck
Text: James Taylor-Foster

Printed in China

The publisher would like to thank Tanya Heinrich, Lisa
Delgado, Susan Clements, and Laura Loesch-Quintin for
their contributions to the book.